D1543129

The Planets

by Martha E. H. Rustad

Consulting Editor: Gail Saunders-Smith, Ph.D.
Consultant: James Gerard
Aerospace Education Specialist
Kennedy Space Center

Pebble Books
an imprint of Capstone Press
Mankato, Minnesota

Pebble Books are published by Capstone Press
151 Good Counsel Drive, P.O. Box 669, Mankato, Minnesota 56002
http://www.capstone-press.com

1 2 3 4 5 6 07 06 05 04 03 02

Library of Congress Cataloging-in-Publication Data
Rustad, Martha E. H. (Martha Elizabeth Hillman), 1975–
   The planets / by Martha E. H. Rustad.
   p. cm.—(Out in space)
   Includes bibliographical references and index.
   Summary: Photographs and simple text introduce the planets in our
solar system.
   ISBN 0-7368-1178-8
   1. Planets—Juvenile literature. [1. Planets. 2. Solar system.] I. Title. II. Series.
QB602 .R86 2002
523.4—dc21   2001004837

Note to Parents and Teachers

The Out in Space series supports national science standards for
units on the universe. This book describes and illustrates the planets
in our solar system. The photographs support early readers in
understanding the text. This book also introduces early readers to
subject-specific vocabulary words, which are defined in the Words
to Know section. Early readers may need assistance to read some
words and to use the Table of Contents, Words to Know, Read
More, Internet Sites, and Index/Word List sections of the book.

Table of Contents

4

Look down at the ground.
You are standing on
a planet. This planet
is called Earth.

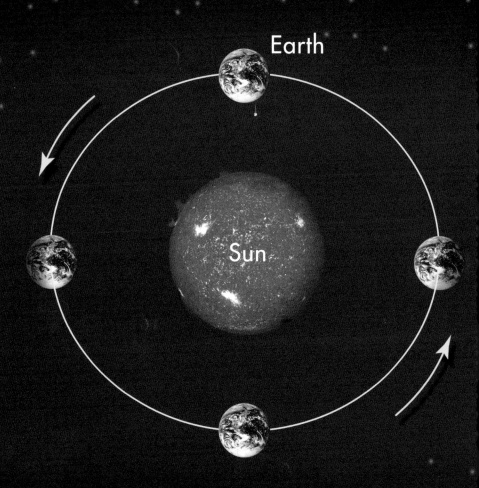

Earth

Sun

A planet is a large object that orbits a star. The closest star to Earth is the sun. Earth orbits the sun once each year.

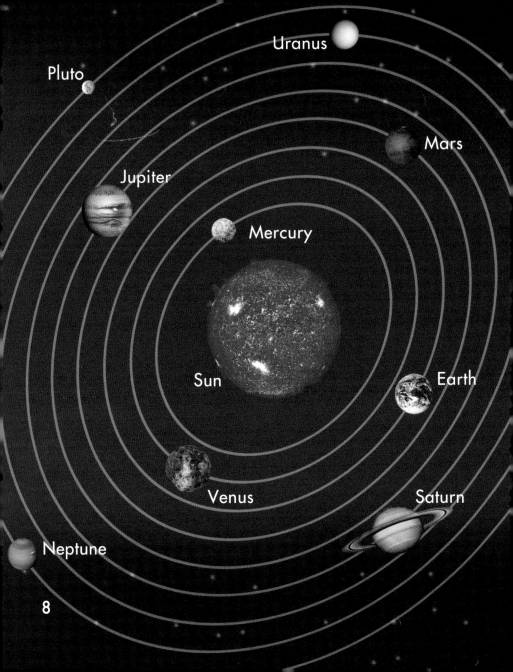

Uranus

Pluto

Mars

Jupiter

Mercury

Sun

Earth

Venus

Saturn

Neptune

8

Earth and eight other planets orbit the sun. The planets and the sun make up the solar system.

Jupiter

Saturn

Uranus

Neptune

10

Jupiter, Saturn, Uranus, and Neptune are large planets. They are made of gases.

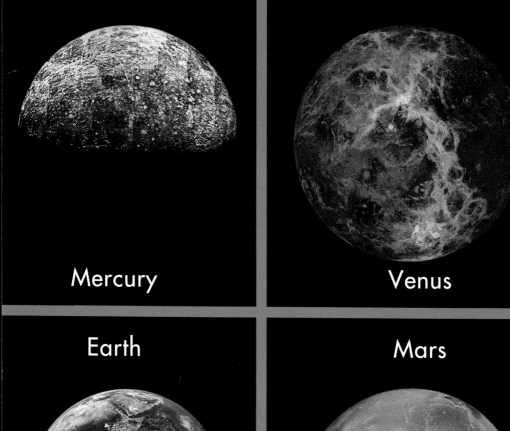

Mercury

Venus

Earth

Mars

12

Mercury, Venus, Earth, and Mars are smaller planets. They are rocky.

14

Pluto is the smallest planet. It is made of rock and ice.

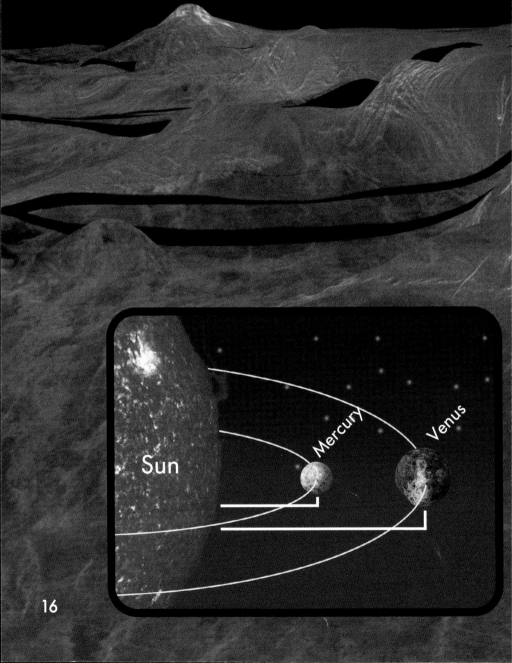

Mercury and Venus are close to the sun. These planets are very hot.

a computer image of the surface of Venus

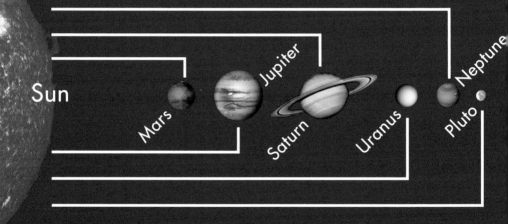

Sun

Mars

Jupiter

Saturn

Uranus

Neptune

Pluto

Mars, Jupiter, Saturn,
Uranus, Neptune,
and Pluto are far from
the sun. These planets
are very cold.

Earth is just the right distance from the sun. People, animals, and plants can live on Earth.

Words to Know

gas—a substance that spreads to fill any space that holds it

orbit—to move around an object in space; Earth orbits the sun in about 365 days, 6 hours.

planet—a large object that orbits a star

rocky—covered in rocks; rocky planets are solid.

solar system—the sun and the objects that orbit it; our solar system has nine planets and many moons, asteroids, and comets.

star—a large ball of burning gases in space; the sun is the closest star to Earth.

sun—the star that gives Earth light and warmth; the sun is about 93 million miles (150 million kilometers) from Earth.

Read More

Dussling, Jennifer. *Planets.* All Aboard Reading. New York: Grosset and Dunlap, 2000.

Gallant, Roy A. *The Planets.* Kaleidoscope. Tarrytown, N.Y.: Benchmark Books, 2001.

Kirkwood, Jon. *Our Solar System.* Look into Space. Brookfield, Conn.: Copper Beech Books, 1998.

Internet Sites

Astronomy for Kids
http://www.astronomy.com/content/static/AstroForKids/default.asp

BrainPOP: Solar System
http://www.brainpop.com/science/space/solarsystem

Welcome to the Planets
http://pds.jpl.nasa.gov/planets

Index/Word List

animals, 21
close, 17
cold, 19
Earth, 5, 7, 9,
   13, 21
eight, 9
far, 19
gases, 11
ground, 5
hot, 17
ice, 15

Jupiter, 11, 19
live, 21
Mars, 13, 19
Mercury,
   13, 17
Neptune,
   11, 19
object, 7
orbit, 7, 9
people, 21
Pluto, 15, 19

rock, 15
rocky, 13
Saturn, 11, 19
solar system, 9
star, 7
sun, 7, 9, 17,
   19, 21
Uranus,
   11, 19
Venus, 13, 17
year, 7

Word Count: 142
Early-Intervention Level: 16

Credits
Timothy Halldin, cover designer and interior illustrator; Kimberly Danger, Mary
   Englar, and Jo Miller, photo researchers

J. Luke/PhotoLink/Photodisc, Inc., 20 (inset)
PhotoDisc, Inc., cover, 1, 4, 6, 8, 10 (top left, top right, bottom right), 12 (all), 16, 18, 20
NASA, 10 (bottom left); Dr. R. Albrect, ESA/ESO Space Telescope European
   Coordinating Facility/NASA, 14